MW01598151

A very special thank you to my friend Chris. The best writer I know and one of the strongest people. To Jacquie for her enthusiasm and the painting she happily donated for the cover. To Eric for turning an already great picture into an epic work of Art. Finally, I thank me for not giving up on myself even though many days I wanted to.

TABLE OF CONTENTS:

Memories of Waiting

That time at Playland when I was eight.
Enjoy the rides. I'll be back at nine.

10:00. I shiver in my paper jacket.

It is last night of the fair in early September.
I wait by the fence near the Pirate Ship,
the picnic area just off to the side
where he told me.
The Banshee howls, a Gremlin waves
from a grove of trees nearby.

10:30. I say hello to Darth Vader,
and allow him to recruit me to the Dark Side
for my own protection.

When you arrive,
I'll go back to being a good young
Christian boy I promise!
The agreement verbal,
not binding,
no documents signed.

11:00. I phone home.
No answer.
I hear the snoring,
silent over the rings,
and postcard cliche I wish I was there.

11:30. He shows up.
Sorry I couldn't be here earlier,
I had important things to take care of.

On the way to the car
I locked my arm in his,
grateful for the closeness,
but then in the darkness,
slightly, very slightly,
my Father pulled away.

Penny-lane

I remember pennies dropping from my
glass jar onto the floor.
Pennylane...memory lane...memories of
pennies.

I was 5 years old.

I wanted comic books.
For weeks I collected loose coins,
did chores,
gathered cash
in the form of pennies.
I didn't like nickels,
dimes, quarters...so insubstantial.
I liked the quantity as it poured,
a river of brown onto the linoleum.

As I have gotten older,
I have slowly started to appreciate
the meaning of pennies.

The clink of brown metal,
like a cell clicking open.

It all comes back to me...5 years old,
brown coins cascading
onto the creaky floorboards,
unaware that the prize
was not really comic books,
rather freedom.

Sleeping Giant

As you lay dying,
a full arena chanted and screamed your name.

He hailed from an era of 300 pound
dead men in black
walking the top ropes
of wrestling rings like acrobats.
Sledge hammer wielding Machiavellians,
clashed with brawling alcoholic rednecks,
while jam packed coliseums brayed for blood.

14 years old,
I watched Air Benoit take flight,
barrel chested ballerina
soaring head first
into rib cage or not.

Sometimes it was the sickening thud
of cranium smacking canvas.

Friday June 22nd, 2007.
Chris Benoit asphyxiated his wife Nancy.
Saturday he asphyxiated his 7 year-old son

Daniel,
left a bible beside both bodies.
Sunday he no-showed
 a company Pay Per View,
instead hung himself from his weight bench,
familiar bible nearby.

The bodies were found Monday afternoon.
That night his wrestling family broke character,
told tearful stories about his life.
He was quiet and gentle. A peaceful man.
Said Daniel was a mini version of him.
That he didn't just love him he adored him.

Benoit's autopsy revealed the mind of an
87 year old Alzheimer's patient
with advanced dementia.

He became the first known case of CTE.
A brain disease,
caused by years of untreated concussions.

When he called Chavo,
said Nancy and Daniel had food poisoning,

did he choke on the words?
Did he almost ask for help?
I've done a bad thing Chavo.
There are goblins in my brain Chavo.
Did his pride prevent him from doing so?

Vince McMahon described what
happened to his family as a tragedy.

Was he referring to lost life or lost dollars?
Was it out of nobility he ordered
his merchandise removed from shelves,
his matches deleted from public domain,
all commentary mentioning him
edited from existence?

Was it out of nobility he made Chris Benoit
the forbidden name of professional wrestling?

Owen Hart fell 30 metres,
and the show went on,
his lifeless body wheeled past other wrestlers.

Difference is when a wrestler dies

they are a tree in the forest.
In comparison,
Nancy and Daniel Benoit
were a car bomb in Central Park.

Steroid use was never established.
Benoit's system was clean,
but Vince implemented
steroid and drug testing.

Those same steroids Vince himself had
used, abused, encouraged.

Anything to extinguish their sound.

Chris we never saw you as human.
You were crash test dummy,
laid low during impact testing.
Underdog superhero,
chiselled to perfection in a pharmacy test tube.

Each squeal of adulation,
driving the needle deeper.

My Delilah (Why Why Why Delilah?)

It was the summer of 1997. I was 19.
You got on at Joyce Skytrain Station.
I fixed you with a quick look of longing.
You smiled as I turned away.

Beautiful night.
Yes. Uh yes...it is.

Not a brilliant start, but the conversation built.
Was your first night in Vancouver.
Had to get away.
Someone had stolen your purse.
You had your paycheck,
but no way to cash it.

You told me how much
you enjoyed my company,
how you wished you could
take me out to dinner.
I suggested you sign the check over to me.
It was for $1500. I could only take out a $1000.
A good excuse to meet tomorrow.

You ensnared me,
in the beam of your searchlight smile.

Several hours later you paid for my cab home,
flung arms around me
through the open car window,
clung to me like a supplication.

Don't let me go, don't ever let me go.
You smelled like a rainbow,
as you kissed me on the forehead,
cheeks, then mouth.
I watched in a daze as the Taxi pulled away.

My.
First.
Kiss.

Next day you had arranged
to view an apartment,
so I left the money in the mailbox
for you to pick up.
You said you would call when you were done.

I waited with 3 red roses,
a small, stuffed Teddy Bear,
and a gigantic box of Nutchos Chocolates,
which I couldn't help sampling.
They were delicious.

The phone never rang.
I dialed through chocolate streaked fingers,
dribbled sticky fingerprints over the cord.
The number you have reached
is not in service.
Again...the number...again...frantic.
Number...envelope was gone.
I devoured entire box of Nutchos.
Check bounced.

You called yourself Jenny,
but you were my Delilah.
Why why why Delilah?

Betrayal hurts that much more
when it awakens a hope in you,
you never knew was missing.

I was despondent for months,
then a strange thing happened.

The euphoria of those hours was real.
Even though our connection wasn't.
I found myself seeking this bliss everywhere.

If it wasn't for your praying mantis
fingers in my pocket,
I may at this very moment be a shut-in,
living in my Mother's basement,
instead of here,
sharing my heart on this stage.

So Delilah, darling, wherever you are,
thank you for saving my life,
in the most unexpected of ways.

Legend of a Hedgehog

Ronald Jeremy Hyatt.
He is the "Porn King,"
Guinness World Record holder for appearing
in over 1800 pornographic films,

100 mainstream TV shows,
movies, and music videos.

Infamously nicknamed the
"Hedgehog" for excessive hairiness
and profuse sweating on set,
this short, squat little man
from the documentary Porn Star:
The Legend of Ron Jeremy
was unexpected.

I expected him to be cold, arrogant, repugnant,
yet Ron exuded an odd warmth,
an awkward charm,
a slightly sad self-deprecation.

He'd always repelled me,
although secretly, I envied him.
Because I'd been with
3 women in my entire life.
Because I mistook sex for intimacy.
Because I always slept alone.

Thing is nobody can escape loneliness.

I wonder when he closes his eyes,
if he can see the face of the
first girl to kiss him.
Or the one who took his virginity.
His first crush.
Perhaps he wrote her a love poem,
crumpled it up,
too terrified to show it to her.

Somewhere in this semen-encrusted Eden,
he fucked his innocence away.
Love became a fairy-tale for schmucks.
An ironic joke.

It is hard to know desire
when every carnal whim is satisfied.
Over time it must blend
into one giant money shot.

There are 3 things
many female porn stars won't do:
Bestiality
Anal sex

Ron Jeremy

He laughs at this.
He likes to make others laugh.
See them smile. See him smile.
See how happy he is.
You have to love him. He makes you laugh.
The biggest porn star in the world.
The fat, ugly little troll,
doing it for the underdog over and over again.

Faithfully fucking the weeks,
the months, the years into oblivion.

Fucking the pain away.
Fucking the pain away.
Fucking his pain away.

Do you hear the snickering...the disdain
in their eyes evident in their touch?

He has fame. He is alone.
He is surrounded by people. He is alone.
He fucks thousands and thousands of women.

He is alone. He has forgotten how to love.
He is trapped in a valley of unholy orifices,
mutant monstrous moans.
The faces are fleshy shadows.
He has forgotten how to love.

There are no more girls to write poetry to.
No more anticipated first kisses.
No cherished faces hidden behind his eyelids.

He has forgotten how to love.

The World Without

I woke up one morning to discover
that the world seemed quieter.
More a feeling than fact.
I turned on TV screen.
Clever banter was craved,
but a white noise squealing
assaulted my ears.
I turned off the screen,
left my apartment.
Up and down alleys blankness assailed
me...billboards wiped stark clean,

signs devoid of words and pictures,

Medleys of colour stripped to a surgical white.

It was as if language had forsaken

its creators. I assailed people

fright-crazed and foaming.

Met with confused token sympathy,

and the grunts of wild ape-men.

Without words we were no better than them.

St. Bumblebee Massacre

My innocence. A

Lily on acid, gang-raped

by honey bees while

too stoned on delusion to

even know the difference.

Sex and the Voiceless

Children:

your parents are having sex.

A LOT.

They're liking it.

Making love exists,

but is for special,

tender occasions.

Your parents are
horny,
humping,
fornicating bunny rabbits.
Learn to like it.

Parents:
one day your child will have sex,
and whether it be love or hate the first time,
Disappointment, confusion,
it will happen again.
Then again.

Many steps towards becoming a
sexually healthy being,
from the innocent kids playing doctor,
to that first unexpected wetness or boner.
But too often answers come
in playground myths.

So you sexual Rapunzels,
let down your golden pubic hair.

These conversations are awkward, sure,
but imagine yourself 15 years-old,
alone in your room,
flogging penis to orgasm,
stock still, dazed by the sudden flow
of semen running down your leg,
onto the sheets.

This is what it feels like to get off.
Sexual education self-taught.
Never did talk about the birds and bees.

As a young boy,
siblings molested by Father,
silently in the dark.
How do you reconcile what you are told
with the actions you sense peripherally?
How do you not loathe yourself
for being offspring of offender?
For any and all sexual desire.
I still struggle with this.

Repression and deniability

is breeding ground for dysfunction.

My parents were also raised in strict,
religious households.
I can't imagine them being
very knowledgeable, happy partners.
I don't excuse my Father,
but he was a very tortured man.

Repression and deniability
is breeding ground for dysfunction.

In 2002 it was estimated 95 percent
of U.S. catholic dioceses
had been undermined by sexual impropriety.
I have little sympathy for
priests molesting altar boys, however,
I can't imagine
spending my entire life
knowing zero of my sexual needs
would ever be met,
never being able to share this part
of myself with anyone.

Repression and deniability
is breeding ground for dysfunction.

Going from confused to monster
is a personal choice,
but we were raised in a
breeding ground for dysfunction.

Children speak to your parents.
Parents speak to your children."

<u>Vancouver Love Poem #1</u>

Vancouver, of beautiful coastline,
mountains, and Stanley Park,
the all-you-can-eat sushi bars,
and yuppieville yaletown,
with the fancy shops,
restaurants,
and nose in the air art critics.

Davie Village,
where the rainbow flag waves proudly,
the stores selling whips,
leather biker outfits,

and edible, multi-coloured condoms.
Where Drag Queens own the clubs,
and men and women,
walk hand in hand with their own sex.
This is somewhere over the rainbow kiddies!

Come out. Watch the residents play,
but keep your prejudices to yourself.

There are passive aggressive hippies
on Commercial Drive,
and poetry slam Monday nights
at Cafe Deux Soleils,
the artsiest of a
string of many artsy coffeeshops.
The Rio Theatre
home to Friday midnight movies,
and my first
Rocky Horror Picture Show experience.

Finally,

there is the 10 block square area around
Main and Hastings,

where all Vancouver's
unwanted children congregate
in a powder keg of nasty.
The alleys are littered with urine,
feces and needles.

The buildings are decrepit,
festering with
benevolent rats and cockroaches.
There's prostitutes on street corners,
begging for tricks at liquidation prices,
and vagrants selling crack rocks for $10.

Having once lived in this neglected corner,
I can state this neighbourhood
fiercely looks after its own,
and adopts all that pass through.

These are Quasimodo's people,
hideous, yet beautiful.

That is one reason I must leave you
Vancouver,
superficially you are beautiful,

but also vain and selfish.
You always need to be world class this,
world class that,
meanwhile you overlook
the sick inside your womb.

Vancouver,
there are cold egocentric edges to your heart.

There is also the constant rain,
and the 2 inches of snow every winter.
What I wouldn't give for a real live blizzard,
and the beauty of cold sunny days in January.

Vancouver,
since 3 years old,
you have been every angry fist and warm hug.
Every drop of laughter and tear to me.
The people who have deliberately hurt me,
and those that have raised candles for me,
brighter than any lighthouse
to help me find my way.

Every shred of my DNA
is tied to your sidewalks,
but 29 years is a long time to ride
this memory roller-coaster.

My first and truest love,
you are the world's most beautiful birdcage,
and the door is slowly closing.
I must fly away
before I am forever locked inside.

Tales from the Hospital Ward #1

I left pieces of myself behind that day.
Petals of plasma sprinkled over pavement
as the ambulance screeched away.

Metal plates a cybernetic gift,
but scar is permanent.
A nine inch kiss of scalpel into skin.

And the intimacy of that touch has lovers'
nuance. Many mornings it flares in memory.

Sometimes I run a tender finger over it.
Transport myself.

When it happened,
I became a 37 year-old man,
reliving 10 year-old boy deja vu.

I came to Vancouver with poems on my lips.
A gaggle of poets mingling,
sharing laughter and lyrics.
Champion wordsmith to be crowned.
Confined to a Hospital bed.
Broken wrist wasn't the only issue.

Something's wrong with your heart.

I was again alone, voiceless,
cowering from my Father.
He'd found my magic wardrobe to Narnia,
and set fire to it.
Murdered Peter Pan in front of me,
buried him in the backyard.
Fed Tinkerbell to the neighbours cat.

As a kid I never had a voice.
So when I finally acquired one,
I ascribed it mystical powers.
The one part of me unable
to be silenced or destroyed.
I would never be powerless again.

On April 26th, 2016 my voice was silenced.
Again powerless.
More afraid than I've ever been.
This terror has not left me.

Since then I've withdrawn to my basement,
rarely come out.
Strangled syllables in a loving death grip.
I can't let myself lose you.

This poem is a venturing out.
A refusal to allow my fear to control me.
The magic wardrobe is intact.
Peter Pan and Tinkerbell are still alive.
Just a bad dream. It's nice outside.
I'm going to sit in the sun.

Snow globe: Apocalypse

I sometimes feel like a
Penguin in a snow globe

after the snow has fallen...As if all the
beautiful parts of my life
have already happened...the memories
as awkward and elusive as the snowflakes
which slipped through my flippers.

I long to dash headlong into brick walls,
jump suicidally off of skyscrapers
for the collision, the rush of air,
the chill of charged adrenaline against skin,
the metallic taste of
wounded life on my tongue.

We are taught about life and death,
but nobody talks about limbo.
That too long purgatory of days,
where the only thing that gets us by
is the monosyllabic crooning of the
voices in our head. *This too shall pass.*

I miss my idealism. When I believed
most people thought for themselves.
There was no such thing as
"hive mind" or "group think."

When every girl that smiled
at me was my next crush,
and every girl I kissed was "the one."

I barely remember my last kiss,
let alone the last kiss that really mattered.
Even the afterglow is a barely accessible haze.

We are all capable of magic as children.

The difference between a Muggle
and a Wizard is that a Wizard
never fully grows up,
never loses the ability to
impose their imagination
on the world around them.

Inside the world of language
there lies a portal of magic and delight.

Each of my pen strokes,
a half remembered spell of invocation.
Years fall off at the edge of the vortex.
I jump inside.

I am 10 years old.
Peter Pan taunting Captain Hook.
Dorothy following the yellow brick road.
The world is Supercalifragelisticexbealadocius!

There are reminders it wasn't all wonderful.
The bullies surround me in the playground,
I once again remember the fear and
isolation of being a childhood outcast.

One by one they attempt to speak...my
pen steals words from their tongue,
flings the insults back at them.
They reach for me,
but their hands now belong to me.
Pants end up around ankles,
wedgies self-induced.

This is what it is to play child god:
World of wonder created without fear.

Writing is the way I shake my snow globe.
Create memories to bask in,
before all that is glorious,
is once again reduced to nostalgia.
And I am alone,
waddling through the aftermath.

Snag & Fade
It is easy to snag sunlight,
to fade into the lazy,
hazy way of loneliness,
punctuated by inertia.

You see depression isn't
cloudy or tempestuous
as most people think, rather,
comfortably, cumulus calm,
familiar, lulling. This is why it draws us.
There is a warm emptiness,
devoid of swirling whirlpools
and luminous madness.

Curtains drawn,
brightness taps on my window pane,
bouncing off this force field of numb.

When was the last time we
closed our shutters on a downpour?
Storms fascinate us, because their
sheer elemental power
enlivens us to a state of caring.

There is a lethargic coziness
in hiding amongst sunlight.
Rocking fetal position,
in need of a thunderstorm.
Give me liquidity,
lightning
and bedlam.

The Making of a Puppet

My silences lack the quietude
that follows midnight snow,
the world blissfully drunk on its own beauty.
They are withheld secrets,

Taut seconds before an explosion of violence.
Quiet nights sleeping alone,
sitting front row center at movie theaters,
so I won't see everybody else is with someone else.
Desperation unspoken.

I worry that every word will spotlight my need.
Every frosty breath in winter
will be smoke signals of desire.

If Pinocchio became a real boy,
than I am becoming Pinocchio.

My trips to Narnia and Wonderland
are longer and more frequent.
I am forgetting how to exist,
turning into a Fairy tale.

In the telling I regain human form,
once again morph into pigment,
skin and bone.

Some days though I am a puppet
with wood chips for a heart,
where blood used to flow.

The Morning After

I sit in a hummy glaze,

the day cast over
with a mist of song
and expectation.

I yearn to see whether you are just some
random Alice,
or the Lewis Carroll Alice,
turning rabbit holes into rapture,
forest gatherings into Narnia.

Where the dangers,
although real are ethereal and wonderful.

Because in this world even death is beautiful,
and I dance on the gravestones of my past

footsteps

the echo of different women,
different times,
joyous for the spot
their memory will always hold.

And I am renewed
amidst these sepulchers,

in the space between raindrops.

Pants-less
Guitar music playing in sunny coffee shop
one Spring evening.

Summer is stalking me,
but it's hard to appreciate warmth,
when you are lacking passion in your life.

I heard recently that Nietzsche
was socially inept,
lone sexual encounter with a prostitute
who gave him syphilis. The thought
makes me feel slightly more functional.

Lesson 1.
If you don't participate in life
it will give you the worst parts of itself.
Lesson 2.
Sometimes,
at least in the case of Nietzsche's legacy,
the worst parts of life
make some pretty tasty lemonade.

I suddenly realize why I prefer
Wile E. Coyote to Roadrunner,
it is his obvious commitment,
fearlessness and ambition.

Knowing he is going to fail in every endeavour,
I still cheer for him, even in truth admire him,
his resolve indomitable, his failures glorious.

He is Rocky Balboa,
minus the World Championships.
The song "eye of the tiger"
was secretly written for him.

But too often I wake up
empathizing with Nietzsche.
The theme song of my life "eye of the kitten."
Anti-Coyote/Balboa,
stopping at the intersection of my life,
looking both ways,
still refusing to cross.

As milquetoast as Geritol and Ovaltine.

The world's meekest,
most socially awkward man,
undisputed king of the mild frontier.

Sometimes I forget.
I forget that I am a member of the
"Brotherhood of the Travelling Pants-less!"
A troupe of emotional poetry exhibitionists,
soul brothers to one Wile E. Coyote Esquire.

Our words are Daredevils,
kamikaze diving into the waiting arms
of some Truth you are desperately ignoring.
Sometimes your denial of this Truth
makes me feel like an isolated anomaly,
but I understand finally.
I am done apologizing for your discomfort.

I hope someday vulnerability will be common.
More poets will write honest poetry,
we'll revere our scars,
instead of hiding from them.

In the meantime I'll continue bleeding,

and do my utmost not to forget who I am.

World Without
My greatest sorrows are acts of omission.
As these butterfly bullet train days
zoom past me,
it seems every
second of wonder is only half wonderful.

Every instant of beauty, less beautiful,
because these moments
contain an element of love, and love
is meant to be shared.

I am a Wolf baying at the Moon,
only to realize that the Moon does not exist.
That it never did.

Broken Pieces
Head nestled into the hollow of a neck,
bare breasts entwining,
fingers gripping buttocks,
the smell of shampoo, perfume,
and semen, drying,

on the inside of dirty jeans,
teeth nibbling on ear,
light tickle of wind,
gyrations more frenetic than the music.

She wants me, she wants me not
She wants me, she wants me not
She wants me...

Dud to stud resuscitation
done in the flash of currency,
but wallet is empty.

Who would ever want you?
Seven years single.
Your ugly's showing.
Like Father,
like Son.

I am not my Father.
You objectify women.
I am not my Father!
You're a predator!
I just want to be wanted!

You know why you have to pay women
to spend time with you?
NO!
Yes yes yes!
NOOOOOOOOOOOO!!!

Growing up, my mom always told me I looked
just like my Father.
Most christian men
don't molest their daughters.
My Father was a christian man.
I looked just like him.

We never talked about sex growing up.
It was a source of shame,
learned through glossy mags
on top shelves of bookstores,
through adult theatre visits,
and blowjob offers
from creepy men in trench coats.

My Father ate for two,
himself and the Demon inside of him.

I ate to make myself
appear as ugly on the outside,
as I felt on the inside.
Yet this side of me was a secret Vampire,
invisible in the mirror of myself
I held up to the world.

The more insidious I felt,
the more I frequented these dark corners.
Friendships and sex,
particularly friendships with women
were inextricably linked.
Inevitably I would think I was in love,
and want to sleep with them.
They always ran away.
I always ran away.

Naked gyrating flesh in dingy clubs,
and oh the mental lashings.
I would say that I no longer know
what healthy sexuality is,
but I never learned in the first place.

It was only 5 years ago I realized I could love a
woman without needing to sleep with her,
that the intimacy of secrets,
and blushing walls sworn to silence
could be more profound
than the swapping of fluids.

So much happiness depends
on not letting the machinery of our lives
run on our broken pieces.

Forgiving the offender is easy.
Forgiving yourself for being a victim;
therein lies the broken pieces.

I write,
because I despise
who I am when I'm not writing.

Poetry is my Aurora Borealis,
my Northern Lights in the wintertime.
Without it, I would be dead,
or insane, (or really, really fucked up),
A cloudy day like now,

but without the sunny periods.

So I will write, I will write, I will write.

Bread Circus

It takes faith to share these lines,
to condemn them to a
world where they may fall empty.
I grip the pen white-knuckled.
This should be easy by now.

Writing words to ward off the empty,
speak them into being,
Sometimes feel even more empty.
A fish without an ocean,
surviving on the droplets of misfits.

I have stated in past writings
that there is a difference
between living your dreams
and living in a dream world.

Which one of those classifications
do I fall under?

Did I dream of being 37 and virtually alone?
Did I dream of being broke
and on the verge of homelessness?
Did I dream that the only thing
scarier than spending my nights alone
would be having someone,
then losing them,
because I was unable to emotionally,
financially provide?

When do sacrifices cross the line
into self-harm?
When am I the pyromaniac
setting fire to my own flesh?
Writing poems about the beautiful way it burns.

After 10 years of running away,
writing found me.
A raw, singular orifice of need,
desperately needing a pen prick to bleed.
I pricked. I bled.
It is impossible to distinguish
the inky waters of love,
from loneliness, from lust.

I am a roiling whirlpool.
The more I bleed,
the more I need rejuvenation.

Shadow people my words have illuminated,
smile at me. *Thank you for seeing me brother.*
I am your kin. Bless you
for shining a light on me."

But sometimes,
all that is illuminated is more darkness.
I am last honeybee in a radioactive world,
last flowers irradiated dust.
Poet in a world of 0% literacy,
where language has never been invented.

There is nothing beautiful about me.
I wouldn't recognize beauty
if it smacked me in the nose with a rainbow.

My philosophy of finding
beauty in the darkness,
just an excuse to wallow in misery.

Words like fearless, courageous, brave,
so laughable.
Why am I afraid of ordinary?
Ordinary job.
Ordinary life,
Ordinary love.

The best of us are never butterflies.
Merely the echo of a butterfly.
Butterfly in love with broken stain glass,
because you don't need
to be perfect to be beautiful,
because it reminds of blood.

We are never more aware of being alive
than when we are bleeding.

What ultimately saves me
from these moments,
my biggest fear,
is not of being alone,
of being forgotten,
of being a fraud or a failure,
my biggest fear is that this maelstrom

will consume me from the inside out,
and I will be indifferent to that fact.

Tales from the Hospital Ward #2

The poke and prod of needles is nothing,
compared to long hours of silence
confined to a surgical bed.

Compared to a statuesque blonde nurse,
cupping your penis and balls in her hand
so you can pee into a bottle,
cheeks flushed from embarrassment,
from shame,
thinking:whatever you do,
do not have an erection,
do not have an erection,
you will renounce any potential belief
in God if you have an erection.

The poke and prod of needles is nothing,
compared to long hours
confined to a surgical bed,
because the flow
of prescription drugs won't stop,

because you are tethered to your IV machine,
because you are too weak to wash yourself.
Once again you succumb to unfamiliar hands,
the cold hands of a stranger.
Clammy alien hands.

The last time you experienced these
levels of intimacy, you had a lover,
before that you were teenager,
first kiss, fumbling,
skin on skin awkward.

Finally, baby,
hands washing you were mother's,
comforting, assured,
before you were aware of body,
shy of touch.

Freedom is unremarkable, overlooked,
until it is taken away,
until you lose control,
until your body becomes
a decaying hovel
you are trapped inside.

Your heart beats too fast,
it has become enlarged. I've been told:
you can't expect a normal heart
to write the kind of poetry you do
or, *looks like your heart*
was broken one time too many.

And it's true,
I've always been too big,
too bumbling, too broken.

Imagine coming awake, realizing,
you are sleepwalking with the scissors
to your life thread.
One snip away from being a chalk drawing,
perpetrator of your own crime scene.

They say a run-in with Death
makes you glad you were alive.
So why did I wish it took me?
That this languid longing lonely had stopped.
My 3 year depression
a passive aggressive suicide.

"I was Happy" said Buffy the Vampire Slayer,
after being resurrected in Season 6.
Torn from some better place.
I am a broken clock.
Standing still.
Lightless lighthouse on choppy water.
This poem doesn't have an ending.

Anonymous
Somebody hung themselves
in the park this morning.
Name, gender, age,
unknown to me.
Only defining characteristic Homosapien.

This same park I've stargazed
and practiced poems in.

My reaction? "How horrible."
A nonchalant and
obligatory expression of remorse.
Such is my desensitization to Death.

Upon reflection I can't help thinking
how this obscurity
christens them Universal Everyman.
How often I've played
Russian Roulette with despair.
How strong the pull to shadows has been.

I can't help but contemplate if my own Death
would be better cloaked in anonymity.
Causing mild intrigue with little grief.
Ghost story. Urban Legend.

My ego wants weeping,
lustful lamentations of mass millions.
Is this the only way I define my worth?

Grief is a natural byproduct,
of making the world better.
Only the most wretched
go unloved and unmourned.
I am not one of these.
The love I have received is why I am still here.

So Dear Anonymous,
even though I lack the means
to mourn you the way you deserve,
I am saddened by your loss.
See your reflection in all I love.
In everybody who has ever felt
this world is too much.

As you fell,
I'm sorry there were no hands to catch you.

Dear Anonymous,
you are me in a less fortunate Time.
I am grateful I have survived
long enough to choose life.

A friend of mine
believes we originally came from a place,
far better than this.
I pray this is true.
One day I hope to meet you there.

I wish you safe voyage across the stars.

The Mortality Diaries

Tonight I hear my own breathing.
Surrounded by 4 walls,
and so much silence,
it seems all other existence
is a waking dream or nightmare.

Tonight I'm not the last survivor
of the Apocalypse,
because life has never lived
outside of me. I am God,
as they may have been at the beginning.

Not a mastermind,
a lonely kid,
wanting someone
to play Tonka Trucks and Barbies with.
Eternal period on a blank page.
No sentence. No Universe. No page.
Just the broken wheeze of my own loneliness.

My internal Wasteland calls and I answer it.
From my tears the forests grow.

Lamplight in the Fog

This poem is not heroic ballad,
larger than life,
conquering hero of hyperbolic virtue.

No feel good happy-ever-after tale.
No cotton candy daydream loaded
with spoonfuls of sugar.

This poem is truth,
first shovelful of dirt,
out of this existential
hole you've buried yourself in.

First lines you've written,
Since numbness braided your hair
singing sweet solace.

It is sad, scarred. scared.
It is loved, longing, lost.

It is the hope you captured,
when the Pandora's Box

in your heart burst open,
when despair overwhelmed,
possessed, controlled you.
Zombie Pinocchio, puppet pratfall,
macabre dancing through the days.

You didn't want to be a real boy though.
You didn't want to be anything.

This poem is lamplight,
lighthouse, but no Saviour.
Searchlight barely cracks through this fog.

Fraying rope over burning volcano,
dilapidated plank on rusty bridge
over hurricane water.

It is tenuous, uncertain, as always your lifeline.

Welcome back Poet I'd like you to stay.

Freaks A-Go-Go

This is a love poem for the ghost dominatrix,

the cyanide-carrot-eating,
suicide-cult-rabbit-children,
hopeless and despairing after the loss of Trix.
The rejects, that the rejects rejected.
Their platform 9 3/4,
has always been those dark corners
they hid themselves in,
to observe,
and escape ridicule.

You know those monsters in the closet,
those creatures under the bed?
They're actually deformed children,
longing to be your friend,
but terrified to be rejected
when you see them with the lights on.

I am one of those deformed children.
Too often, I've played fly to the spatula,
careening into walls, my wings
bruising so badly,
I was afraid to soar.
As I grew older,

my weirdness grew
in symmetry with my resilience.

I became a junkyard, tin-can moth,
stained-glass barbed wire butterfly,
clueless to my acquired beauty,
as I long ago learned to fear mirrors.

I encounter my glory,
mirroring off the wings of another,
but don't recognize it.
I discover love, but am oblivious.
I don't understand intimacy,
without the presence of bloodshed.

I am all love parcels and doubt bondage.
Kitten fluff erotica,
instead of snuff film macabre hardcore.
I long to take to stages,
with the manic zeal of a suicide bomber,
all Hippie, word-bomb slinging,
Hallelujah rapture.

I long for this fearless love,

this tornado-breath ambivalence,
this poetry-ripping hyperbole bravado.

My voice issues from my heart,
my heart expands every time I speak.
One day it will encompass the world.
But today it is barely big enough for my chest.

Vancouver: Love Poem #2

Trans Canada Highway November 2011.
Highway closed due to a snowstorm.
I venture outside the Greyhound
and like a little child gaze skyward,
before catching snowflakes on my tongue.

I encounter a blonde-haired,
hippie version of Orlando Bloom.
We look at each other, smile.
I ask him his name.
"Time."
"Wow, cool name. Do you call yourself that to remember
the importance of using your time wisely?"
"Kind of...well more as a reminder not to exist."

We talk a bit more, I perform a poem.
"Whoa Spoken Word is your surfboard."

Initially, I thought this meeting meant things
would happen in their own time and place,
but when my Dad died in January,
the message changed:
The only time guaranteed is the Now.

There is a lot I love about Vancouver.
From big bang poetry with Carl Sagan
baking apple pie,
to Beauty Babo Butterflies
fucking on warheads,
flying pigs masturbating,
on bacon-filled mushroom clouds,
and barefoot Hippie men,
writing love poems to their vaginas.

There is all day breakfasts at Bon's,
the fall days rolling,
giggling in leaves,
with my best friend Zoe,
the leaves all but disappearing,

as they mingle with her red hair.

The wild roller coaster ride of always
falling in and out of love,
the rise of euphoria,
the heart smash taste of twisted metal.

Skeletons of memory stalk me
with their bloody footprints,
wrap themselves around me,
like a cocoon of umbilical cords.

Vancouver is like the open arms
of the girl next door
I always imagined I would marry.
Now grown up,
the butterflies have deserted me.
I no longer crave that white picket fence,
2 car garage,
overly affectionate Labrador Retriever,
tongue lolling out the window of the SUV.

My life was never meant to be safe,
but somehow it became this.

Safety too often means dependence,
dependence means chains,
chains are connected to cages.
Eventually,
you learn to pick locks,
and like Houdini I played "escape artist."

I was sick of being a cuckoo bird
in a tiny cage, of the corpses of addiction,
jumping Zombie style out of burial plots.

The ghost of my Father,
is one I am finally ready to release.
Along with my Mother's doubts,
her "you will never be successfuls"
a giant Albatross anchor around my neck,
tripling in weight,
on the days when failure
brought me back to her door.

But I shall no longer play the Ancient Mariner.
I will not drown in the middle of the Ocean,
with the curse of her disbelief around my neck.

I will take my words, and use them
ala Silver Surfer, to glide through my reality.

Here in Ottawa, I am finally home.
That place where I am travelling
towards something,
I know not what,
but my Heart knows it is an Adventure,
and most definitely will not be safe.

To Dream or Not to Dream
"See what dreams will get you?"
My brother James
holds up a green one dollar bill
with the words Bank of the Bahamas on it.

I suppress a shudder.
We are cleaning out my Dad's apartment.
He died less than two weeks ago.
This appears to be his lone monument
to the wealth he many times declared
would soon be his.

I wish to make a distinction,

that perhaps he was chasing
the wrong kind of wealth,
while mistreating his family,
and therefore ended up with nothing.
but his apartment speaks for him...filth, rot,
the stench of urine and rotted floorboards,
and junk holding up junk,
each broken in such a way that they
fit together and support the other.

As if each inanimate object had figured out the
formula for the continuation of the human race.

"Just don't be broken in the same places."

My Father was a dreamer...I am a dreamer,
my Brother's words hit me a little hard.
"See what dreams will get YOU."

The message in the slight inflection.

The sparseness of language like poetry...and
I once again remind myself that there is a
difference between living your dreams,

67

and living in a dream world.

A modern day Nero,
fiddling as your Rome burns.
"Wake up,
you are not a wheeling and dealing billionaire,
nor a Rockstar in a Spoken Word Band.
Wake up!
You are a Father and your family is burning!

Too late though,
the land of dreams has claimed you,
All that remains is ashes,
scattered over your birthplace,
and the fires you left behind.

We were bonded by dreams,
but I don't dream of wealth and power.
Occasionally, I imagine being famous,
but most times I am grateful
for the friends I do have.

I share some of my Father's same
recklessness...his

lifestyle chosen by his
intense desire for money.
Mine by an attempted disdain.

Sometimes, I imagine my friends,
standing in a circle, chanting:
"You are a man, and your past is burning,
leave the land of poetry and come back to us!"

"You are a man, and your present is burning,
leave the land of poetry and come back to us!"

"You are a man, and your future is burning,
leave the land of poetry and come back to us!"

This is where we differ the most Father.
You led your life for future happiness,
future riches,
ignoring and abusing
all the things in your current life,
that could potentially make you happy.
Not always,
but most times I am happy for what I have,

more importantly who I have.
This is riches enough.

If society's version of my life burns,
I never wanted to live it in the first place.
My true friends would be there,
dancing around the bonfire.

"Yes Jimmy, that's what dreams will get you."
I turn away and risk a hidden smile.

Open Letter:
To the Beds that have borne me:

Dear beds,
receptacles of excess,
you containers of deodorant-free fluff,
domiciles of drool,
holders of flatulence,
chaste victims of more bare-assed hi-jinx,
than any ghetto encrusted
toilet seats anywhere.

Thank you for your patronage,

catching crumbs and cradling,
weeping naked flesh on too many nights alone.

Thank you for long suffering silence,
for mere whisper of springs
after constant defilement.

Apologies for the acts of solo loving,
and the evidence left on your body.

I don't envy you your job,
professional snuggler, surrogate,
substitute partner,
comfortable dream maker,
wet dream,
morning wood taker.

You are the accomplice of all
my procrastinations and laziness,
the confidante of all my tears.
You have always been my perfect refuge,
my rejuvenation,
my makeshift hospital when I am sick.

It has been many years
since I have jumped on your bedsprings,
enjoyed the happy squeal of your mechanics
beneath my bare feet. I am bigger now,
and I don't wish to break you,
but it has been eons since I've heard you sing.

Metallic soprano,
may this poem be an opera,
with you a one woman band,
I have always considered myself
a one woman man.

Yet I love you, and this is not enough,
so call me your poly-amorous,
filth and semen encrusted Dan Juan,
for I am seeking one more to
help your box-spring belt again,
one more to spoon when I look out
the window at a sunrise,
one more to write poetry to.

Autobiography of a Body
I am what you are most terrified of becoming.

I was once a little boy so hungry for love,
I devoured everything edible as substitute.
At the same time I was building a fortress,
my own little "Castle on a Cloud"
out of layers of lard,
to keep the ugliest parts of the world out.

But this creation took over,
moulded its curves and sinews to my body,
locked me inside.

As I grew older I quickly learned
that my safe haven,
this self-mutilation by way of digestion,
was more of a target than a refuge.

The taunting, chanting of names,
rabid bloodletting was palpable.

I made Fat jokes so people would laugh.
I made Fat jokes,
because if people were laughing at me,
people weren't hurting me.

This is why my Fat is jovial,
Fat is clown.
Fat is terrified of everybody,
because Fat is alone.

My first crush Beth Prediger,
(all freckles, blonde hair, sunlight),
turned me down flatter than a jock's six pack,
when I asked her to dance
at Grade 7 Graduation.
I don't want to be seen with you.

Stay away,
take the loneliness away.
Burn this body down,
melt my Fat away.
Flames extinguished by the waterworks.

Now,
as a man who has struggled
his whole life to accept himself,
I have a message for all those
who have judged and tormented me.
For all those in the future who will do so.

I no longer ask for your acceptance.
I will no longer make a mockery of my identity,
in a desperate attempt to gain your love.
During these long,
painful years of self-discovery,
I have known love,
from far better people,
than you could ever hope to be.
You are not worth my time.
I do not wish to know you.

To my friends,
who accept and love me as I am,
to all who will accept and love me in the future.
The scared little boy is still there.
I want you to know this.

I see him when I study myself
too long in the mirror.
To this day eye contact terrifies me.
I can't bring myself to ask a woman out,
risk that familiar sting of rejection.

The major difference is most times
I believe it is possible for people to like me.
Some days I even believe I am beautiful.
On a good day
I believe I am worthy of being loved.
At my best I even love myself.
But this self worth is as fragile
as gossamer wings.

On the days I can not muster
any of these things,
I ask you love me.
Sing a lullaby of healing to this shattered,
catatonic little boy inside of me.
Remind me how beautiful I am.
Sometimes I forget.

Down The Rabbit Hole

I've always been an addict.
My addictions masquerade,
as a whisper of comfort in the darkness.

But whether I am cradling
human time bombs to my chest,

or turning glutton to feed the icy sea inside me
this is the way I plug that aching hole in my gut
which is leaking Stardust.

So it was my friend Peter
taught me to count cards.
Said he needed a partner to get rich with.
Companion to chase dreams
on 5 am nights,
the clinking of slot machines
our obscene private mardi gras.

We were lost in the mire of odds and bet.
Caught in the glamour of lights and machine,
the pursuit of purpose.

Our mission to create a stack of money
so large it would drown our self-loathing,
from this point onward,
a towering pillar of wealth and success.

This is how broken Adults see Wonderland.
In furtive glimpses, with massive regrets.

We are skittish Alices,
our white rabbit a thrilling,
chaotic lover, which goes by many names,
but is most notable for its
aftertaste of despair, this dog collar
around our neck it chokes us with,
simultaneously whispering promises of better.

And we listen. We want so badly to believe.
Our 7 year old brain compels us.
For some of us,
this spiral of dysfunction is a childhood toy,
an old coat, familiar,
as hot cocoa in winter.

For 5 years of my twenties I counted to 21,
lost count of cash coin slipping through fingers.

I once bee-lined from
Gambler's Anonymous to Blackjack.
$200 only thing warding off my eviction.
Talk had been an aphrodisiac.
Just needed a quick fix,
a quick, passionate fuck with the white rabbit.

Get my rent money.

As usual I couldn't quit,
as usual these piles of chips
didn't make a dent in my ocean of loneliness.
As usual broke and broken. Ashamed.
More wretched than I walked in.

That night I aimlessly wandered
East Vancouver wastelands.
5am found me at my Mother's door.
After a sobbing argument I moved back home.

Bad is constantly taking advantage
of the person who loves you more
than anyone else in the world.
Worse is owning up to it.
Worst is seeing they still love you.
You hate them for this love,
you don't deserve it.
You'll never be able to repay it.
You'll never know how to love this way.

These days my white rabbit is poetry.

I get high off the healing she brings me.
We are all addicts.
Charter members of Lifeaholics Anonymous,
seeking purpose and redemption.
I see you. Hiding in the shadows.
I still linger there.
Have never stopped being one of you.
You are not alone.

Revenge of the Ant People

Sometimes it strikes out of nowhere.
This ant looking up to see boot
descending moment.
As if every dreamer that has ever dreamed,
chose this exact moment
to give up on their dreams,
and I am caught in the psychic backlash.

The Universe whispers into my ear:
You are a speck of dust.
And for the first time I am
self-aware enough to hear it.

But stubborn ant that I am,
I grab a pen,
use it to pole vault out of the way
of the in-coming boot,
then stab it repeatedly,
into the Universe's windpipe.

I use the fountain of blood as ink,
to write this poem.

Dear Universe,
Fuck you!
This little speck of dust is going to rally
other specks of dust and create dust storms.
Sincerely,
D.M.P. (Daniel Mark Patterson).

The first step to conquering your demons is
naming them.

Some of them are assigned
like Guardian Angels.
Others are universal. These succubi of dread
slide into the sighs in our bones and feed.

Masters of mirage and shadow,
they are vulnerable to sunlight,
arm yourself with friends
who see the good in you,
their words will illuminate,
even when they are not around,
poking holes in the miasma.

When confronted do not run,
scream your mantras of positivity into the fog.
Do the silliest thing you can think of,
then laugh at yourself.

Carl Sagan said we are all made of stars.
Realize also that we are all made of scars.
Each scar a story, and a lesson,
as divine and wonderful
as all that shimmers within us.

As much scardust as stardust.
As artists we are part teacher,
part star-dancer,
both Astrologer and Priest.

Our religion the exhibition of beauty,
the pursuit, observation and creation of it.
Our purpose, to free it,
from whatever enemies trap and enslave it.
Our words slay Jabberwockies.

Come with me friends,
it is Jabberwocky hunting Season,
and they make damn good eating.
CHARGE!!!

Midnight in a Perfect World

It's midnight in a perfect world,
and it's raining meteorites and jack o' lanterns.

The Wicked Witch of the West and her flying
monkeys have invaded the White House.
Superman has disintegrated
in a kryptonite shower.
The Kremlin is at war
with the Oompa Loompas.

Pinky and the Brain
have taken over North Korea.

The Care Bears have conquered China,
turning their entire nuclear arsenal
into Skittles and jelly beans.

Batman and the Joker admit their love,
and go on a crime spree,
stopping in Canada,
just long enough to hijack a Priest
and get married.

Yosemite Sam captures Bug Bunny,
turns him into rabbit stew.

It's midnight in a perfect world.

Dorothy is now a heroin addicted porn star.
Scarecrow is serving life for molesting children.
Tin Man's heart malfunctions,
he's a serial killer.
Toto is living out his golden years
in a puppy mill.
Cowardly Lion's skin
is hanging on Auntie Em's wall.

It's midnight in a perfect world.

Wile E. Coyote falls off one cliff side too many.
Daffy Duck has a fatal overdose
in his own Warner Bros. theme park.
Cinderella and Prince Charming get a divorce.
So much for happy-ever-after.

It's midnight in a perfect world.

At a young age we are taught gravity,
is merely an inconvenience,
that water and flying houses will defeat,
even the most formidable of villains.
Follow the yellow brick road.
Find your happy-ever-after.

But then we fall,
gravity reasserts its dominance,
water does nothing to
melt the lust of groping hands.
Sometimes a pumpkin is just a pumpkin.
There are demons on the yellow brick road,
salivating, feasting on dreams, hopes, skin.

Midnight is the time when the last of our
childhood illusions are stripped away.
At 12:01, we decide
what new lies to tell our children.

Celebratory Madness

You seem fine said the nurse practitioner.
As if it didn't take me years of
fear, anxiety, depression,
to extend a trembling hand.

As if all of us who are broken,
flash this in neon lights on our forehead.
As if we don't camouflage
our vulnerability to survive.

"You're intelligent and articulate.
You have a good sense of humour."

She never saw the hours and days
hiding in my room,
because I didn't want to face the other people
living in the same house.

Never mind the outside world.

The number of times
I've rehearsed this conversation.
The tremor in my throat as I
force out the words
I'm not coping. I haven't been for a long time.

It takes a year of pleading,
before I get an assessment.
The psychologist eyes me like an exotic insect.

His diagnosis takes minutes:
Severe depression,
severe anxiety disorder,
severe social avoidant personality disorder.
Describes me as cold, emotionless,
lacking empathy.
Robotically rattles off the traits of a
psychopath.

In actuality I disassociated myself,
hid my emotions away
as he took a meat cleaver to the sacred,

dropped pieces of personality in neat,
tidy boxes.

I laughed, silently, bitterly,
as he said
I would never be able to speak in public,
my lack of emotions would stop me
from ever truly being able to fall in love,
from ever developing close friendships
with other human beings.

I never told him about the years
of Theatre and Spoken Word.
Kept the car crash heartbreak to myself.
Never told him about those friends
I loved so fiercely,
the times that love saved my life.

Truth is even though I was a
long way from understood,
part of me was just happy to be finally seen.
My dysfunction displayed like a merit badge.

How do we know you're disabled? Prove it.

The jurors
scrutinize me for hunched shoulders,
lack of dignity, obvious weakness.
Where is your stammer? Remove request.
Replace it with a grovel.

For 3 years I fell through the
titanic fault-lines of this system,
my less than, not less enough,
my destitution too hopeful.

The letter finally arrived:
"Congratulations,
you have been found permanently disabled."
As if was something to celebrate.
You're
Super-calla-fragilistic-exbe-broke-a-docius,
even though the sound of it
is something quite atrocious,
you're
super-calla-fragilistic-exbe-broke-a-docius!
Congratulations you lucky few,
you lowest of low,
your failures are fully documented.

Dance with stooped shoulders,
dance without joy,
dance with surrender in your heart,
slower, get that spry out of your step,
that glimmer out of your eye.

Yes. Excellent. Excellent.
Bravo. Job. Well. Done.

Things to remember on a bad day
Sometimes you have to let the sweetness out.
It is hard to properly love yourself
when you are broken hearted,
choking, on the bitter expectation
of who you imagined yourself to be.

The Hallelujah chorus
is alive inside your chest.
It is just buried under a
rotten pile of fruit and regret.
Excavate your Fandango green midnights,
your monarch butterfly tap dance choir,
your marching band of Latin lovers

drunk on the innocence of
never having your heart broken.

Your memory of destruction
needs to be as short
as your memory of beauty,
or ugliness has won.
Adorn yourself,
in the 25 best moments of your life.

You are a Broadway musical celebration.
A Julie Andrews solo. A ticker tape parade.

Sometimes you have to let the sweetness out,
or the atrophy gets inside.
Even your Birthday parties
become tooth decay and indigestion.
Nobody loves a curmudgeon.
Stop being the creepy miser in the corner.

Be a better friend. Hold yourself at 3am.
Stop curb stomping your face
into the pillow case.

Cry beautiful, cry ugly,
weep until the oceans of water
that make up your body
become a barren desert.

Have phone sex with your answering machine.
You are your most important intimate partner.

Never ask what you have
to offer someone else.
You are Aurora Borealis on a clear night.
What bonfire fireflies,
honey bee flower sonatas do they bring?
Just talking to you is intimidating. Be gracious.

Stop setting yourself ablaze.
You are not a forest fire.
You are a sapphire galaxy on blast furnace.

Even deities have bad hair days.
Even superheroes get crotch rot.
Even galaxies have pesky black holes,
pulling them inside out.

Sometimes you have to let the sweetness out.

You are the tornado puppet master.
Weaver of your own Solar System.
Put on a loose fitting pair of pajamas
and black hole vacuum
your useless stars away.

You are your own perfect world.
There is no midnight.
Stop giving yourself Kryptonite injections.
You are the second most wonderful
creature in my Universe,
and I would love to spend time
exploring it with you.

When the Writing Stops

There are days I talk about greatness,
as if it was a falling star alighting on my hand.
See the value of my words,
importance of following dreams,
inexplicable to most.
But times like now,
in between creations,

those moments pen ceases to move,
playing 9-5 game of survivalist society,
work job, get by, just get by.
I feel like a black hole,
sucking good out of this world.
Every karma dollar borrowed,
a debt to universe.
Logistically, not worth having around.

These days such a struggle
to drag shell of a body out of bed.
Siren song of the blanket,
more insistent than call to face another day.
Close my eyes,
soak up comfort of oblivion, retreat,
can't help wish it were permanent,
only to be returned to this
state of almost wakefulness,
again and again, until sighing,
drag myself upwards like a curse.

Haul myself into work cubicle,
try to matter enough people will tell me
about political preferences,

how much money they make,
their favourite colours, or toothpaste.

I wish God were on the calling list.
So God on a scale of 1 to 10,
how do you feel about
your job creating the Universe?
Come to think of it...outside of the Big Bang
what have you really caused
in the last few Billion years?
Does this creative block make you a has been?
And if we are created in your image,
does that make you as fucked up as we are?
I'd feel better knowing the almighty was fallible,
had insecurities,
perhaps cut myself a little slack.

I tell myself I'll never write again.
Without words I am petty, spiteful, mean.
My normally sincere congratulations of friends'
achievements are saturated with envy.
I imagine growing fangs,

snapping them closed in a
death grip on their arm.
Sucking worthiness out as if
my tongue were a straw,
and goodness a tangible fluid.

I wish to think I'm better than this,
not entirely sure it is true.
Distract myself with mundane tasks
until weary eyes close,
exhausted from the effort of being open.

I forget what starlight is,
so removed from all that is good,
nothing but shadows greet me
in this waking tomb.

Approach my mirror,
expectant of having sprouted horns and a tail.
Convinced I'm Lucifer,
these blank pages were Heaven.
Now I've arrived in Hell.
A cocoon of indifference and stagnation.

But always against all hope
I find myself back at writing desk.
Stanzas trickle out my veins,
into the pen, onto the page,
until they become rivers of ink.

Purpose once again infuses.
Siren song of the mattress fades.
I am not whole,
rather I have again embarked
on this quest for wholeness.
Only time I ever truly fell in love
was with poetry.
Wish I could hold on to my faith
she will never leave me.
Without her a wretched thing.

Confessions of a Body

I am a consumer.
Burger or potato chips in one hand,
enabling words in the other.

I consume large pizzas,
I consume all-you-can-eat sushi,

I consume literal tubs of ice cream.

This food is a buffer,
both a way to keep the world out,
and absorb as much of it as possible.

I am simultaneously creating an
impenetrable fortress out of my body,
while ingesting enough of the world,
there is no longer room for my empty,
my lonely, my broken.

But these hollow places inside me
expand at the same rate,
are now gaping maws,
and no matter how much I eat
I can't hide from them.

But still I gorge, I feast, I devour.

I use positive lessons about body image
"Love yourself"
"you're perfect just the way you are"
"don't body shame"

as an excuse to victimize my body,
demolish my skin,
arson my veins ablaze.

But denial is a poor nemesis for truth.
Often my heartbeats gallop out of control,
tiny excursions turn into
labouring, gasping marathons.
Getting out of bed too quickly
causes shortness of breath.

Yesterday, I couldn't find a big enough seat
in a food court.
A group of kids nearby giggled hysterically.
I still have no idea if they were laughing at me.

I am in an abusive relationship with myself,
committing insidious mutilations,
behind a fake veneer of love.

I will not stop. I don't know how to.
I'll try to be aware and do it less.

A child picks up almost everything they see.

I only ever learned how to harm myself.
I still have no idea how to help myself,
what that even means
outside of vague abstractions.
I won't be here long if I don't figure it out.

This poem is a confession.
Within its lines I am brave.
Within its lines
I am the most honest I have ever been.
Within its lines I am the
warrior I've always wanted to be.

I worry about what happens
when I leave this stage.
When the syllables stop.
When I have no metaphors to hide behind.
Whether I can find the poetry to change.

Across the Universe

So upon reflection,
in my quest for gratitude
I would like to thank poverty

for consistently having my back,
keeping my addictions in check.

Those nights when a never ending
gutter stupor seemed preferable
to sober nights alone.

When Mr. Jack Daniels
seemed like the kindest lover
a lonely poet ever had,
and Edgar Allen Poe's ghost
the most soulful drinking partner.

When I am pulled out of this need
for indulgence by the realization
that an alcoholics lifestyle
is way out of my price range.

That dear Edgar's ghost
was far more of an aristocrat,
a jetsetter, than poor poet I.
This epiphany is both galling and hilarious.
Most days I don't regret my choices.
Freedom is a rich person's currency,

and just ask Judas Iscariot
pining away in Hell,
how many bags of silver was it worth
not to have sold my artistic soul to Capitalism?

Although then at least I could afford
cheap beer to drown my sorrows
about an empty bed,
and trading quips with a legendary
gutterite's ghost is its own reward.

Usually though I would take who I am,
insecurities and all,
Grateful for these words,
this great spongy hug of syllables
to wrap my existence in.

I am lucky enough to narrate my own life,
no frills and gimmick free.
So let the cool kids have their gutter,
their alcoholic, jetsetter, socialite free-for-all.
Just give me the language
to chronicle this night,

this throbbing, endless yearning,
amidst this ocean of stars.

So thankful for the ability to write this poem,
to tell others I was here, tiny, alone, but I loved,
believed in beauty, in more than myself.

When the Starpeople
come...my cosmic soulmate
will recognize me by the journal
buried in my coffin.
Papyrus cracked and yellow,
beside my crumpled sack of bones.

She'll find a love poem,
which only she can appreciate,
pour herself a glass of wine,
curl up to smiling dreams of DeLoreans,
the number 88,
and misfit lovers
years and worlds apart.

Alliterative Litterings

Sometimes I don't write,

sentences don't flow,
no syllables, slip, slippery, sliding,
no tongue twisters,
page plunging, pirouetting,
no alliteration acrobats,
no dervishly dancing devils,
masterful metaphorical musings,
resplendent, radiant, raw.

Do not call this writer's block.

I don't write, because I'm afraid,
of what I will force out.
The lineage of heartache,
hunger, loneliness, lust,
resides in brittle bones.

I fear their expulsion,
not just for what they'll unleash,
but how lonely I'll be without them.
My precious demonic denizens
are the only ones that have never left me.

In the darkness even monsters
can be beautiful.
In the darkness it is so much easier to lie.
In the darkness there are no expectations.

The light is luminous lovely.
The light is terrifying truth.
The light is a harbinger of transformation.

I fear I no longer belong there.
I fear changing.
I fear being completely alone.

So sometimes I can't bring myself to write,
cuddle my creature friends close,
close the windows,
turn off the lights,
reside where the shadow people are.

Sometimes I write a poem,
pensive, pen pounding into page
and the shadows infinitesimally lessen.

Pen pricks of light. Starlight on my ceiling.

Made in the USA
Monee, IL
10 November 2019

16592509R00059